T0083157

Creation Song

Bob Chilcott

for upper voices, SATB, and organ

vocal score

MUSIC DEPARTMENT

OXFORD
UNIVERSITY PRESS

OXFORD
UNIVERSITY PRESS

Great Clarendon Street, Oxford OX2 6DP,
United Kingdom

Oxford University Press is a department of the University of Oxford.
It furthers the University's objective of excellence in research, scholarship,
and education by publishing worldwide. Oxford is a registered trade mark of
Oxford University Press in the UK and in certain other countries

© Oxford University Press 2021

Bob Chilcott has asserted his right under the Copyright, Designs
and Patents Act, 1988, to be identified as the Composer of this Work

First published 2021

Impression: 4

All rights reserved. No part of this publication may be reproduced,
stored in a retrieval system, or transmitted, in any form or by any means,
without the prior permission in writing of Oxford University Press

Permission to perform this work in public (except in the course of divine worship)
should normally be obtained from a local performing right licensing organization,
unless the owner or the occupier of the premises being used already holds
a licence from such an organization. Likewise, permission to make and
exploit a recording of these works should be obtained from a
local mechanical copyright licensing organization

Enquiries concerning reproduction outside the scope of the above
should be directed to the Music Rights Department, Oxford University Press,
at music.permissions.uk@oup.com or at the address above

ISBN 978-0-19-354586-1

Music and text origination by Katie Johnston
Printed in Great Britain on acid-free paper by
Halstan & Co. Ltd, Amersham, Bucks.

Contents

Movement 1	5
Refrain 1	8
Movement 2	9
Refrain 2	10
Movement 3	11
Refrain 3	13
Movement 4	14
Refrain 4	16
Movement 5	17
Refrain 5	20
Movement 6	21
Refrain 6	23

Composer's note

Creation Song was written as a response to a request from Ashley Grote, the Master of Music at Norwich Cathedral, along with Canon Aidan Platten from the Dean and Chapter. Norwich Cathedral was due to be the final stop on a nationwide British tour, which began in February 2018, of the replica skeleton of 'Dippy' the dinosaur from the Natural History Museum in London. The idea was to celebrate this visit to Norwich with a piece that could be sung by the Cathedral Choir along with a large choir of schoolchildren. The resulting work, *Creation Song*, is scored for upper voices, SATB, and organ. It is written in sections with a recurring refrain but is designed to be sung as a continuous piece. The opening tempo marking suggests a speed that remains constant throughout, but please feel free to allow for some flexibility of tempo in certain sections if that feels right to you. The refrain, written for upper voices, can equally be sung by the mixed choir in any voice combination that you may choose should an upper-voice choir not be available. I am grateful to both Ashley Grote and Canon Aidan Platten, as well as the Norfolk Music Hub, for the commitment, energy, and enthusiasm that they have shown towards this lovely project.

Duration: *c.*12 minutes

A lyric sheet and separate part for the upper voices is available for free download from the catalogue page of the OUP website.

Commissioned by the Dean and Chapter of Norwich Cathedral with generous support from the Norfolk Music Hub, for the Natural History Museum's 'Dippy on Tour' exhibition in Norwich, and in celebration of the beauty of creation as the world seeks a sustainable future.

Creation Song

BOB CHILCOTT

Movement 1

Genesis 1: 1–5 (adap.)

© Oxford University Press 2021

Printed in Great Britain

OXFORD UNIVERSITY PRESS, MUSIC DEPARTMENT, GREAT CLARENDON STREET, OXFORD OX2 6DP

The Moral Rights of the Composer have been asserted. Photocopying this copyright material is ILLEGAL.

11
p
pp
form, and void, void; and dark-ness was up - on the
p
pp
p
pp
15
p
face of the deep, deep. And God
p
p
19
ff
said, Let there be light: and there was light.
ff
ff

23
p
And God saw the
p
p
27
mp
mf
light, that it was good. And God called the light Day,
mp
mf
mp
mf
31
mp
p
and the dark - ness he called Night.
mp
p
mp
p
attacca

Refrain 1

Thomas Traherne (*c.*1637–1674)

Movement 2

Joseph Addison (1672–1719)

Refrain 2

Thomas Traherne (*c.*1637–1674)

Movement 3

Isaac Watts (1674–1748)

11
sing the good - ness of the Lord, who filled the earth with
I sing the good-ness of the Lord, who filled the earth with
14
mf
food, who formed the crea - tures through the Word, and
food, who formed the crea - tures through the Word,
mf
mf
17
mp
then pro-nounced them good, good, good.
mp
and then pro-nounced them good, good, good.
mp
attacca

Refrain 3

Thomas Traherne (*c.*1637–1674)

Movement 4

Gerard Manley Hopkins (1844–89)

12
p
mp
Look, look at the stars! The bright bo - roughs, the cir - cle -
mp
15
-ci - ta - dels there, cir - cle - ci - ta - dels there! Look at the
p
p
18
stars, look at the stars, the stars!
attacca

Refrain 4

Thomas Traherne (*c.*1637–1674)

Movement 5

Emily Dickinson (1830–86)

13
mf
tune with-out the words
And ne - ver, ne - ver,
mf
17
f
ne - ver stops at all, at all.
f
f
Man.
20
mf
And sweet-est in the gale is heard;
And sore must be the storm That
mf
Ped.

24
lit - tle bird
mp
could a - bash the lit - tle bird, the lit - tle bird That
mp
mf
mp
Man.
Ped.
27
p
kept, that kept so ma - ny warm,
p
p
Man.
31
rit.
that kept so ma - ny warm.
rit.
Ped.

Refrain 5

Thomas Traherne (*c.*1637–1674)

Movement 6

Thomas Traherne (*c.*1637–1674)

6
which sa - lute mine eyes A gift from
re - gions which sa - lute mine eyes, from
which sa - lute mine eyes A gift from God, from
- lute, sa - lute mine eyes A
8
ff
God I take, from God, from God I take.
God I take, from God I take, from God I take.
God, from God I take, from God, from God I take.
gift from God, from God I take, from God I take.
ff
attacca

Refrain 6

Thomas Traherne (*c.*1637–1674)

12
a little slower
ff
skies, The sun and stars are mine, the sun and stars are mine, if those I
ff
day, the skies, The sun and stars are mine, if those I
ff
a little slower
ff
17
fff
prize, if those I prize, if those I prize.
fff
prize, I prize, I prize, prize.
fff
fff